TESTIMONIALS

Rich is a person that has been given great talents. He has a love for Jesus and teaching His word and living out God's word while remaining very humble. Plus, his desire for all of God's children to come and know him and live the life God has planned for them would make this a great read.

Michael Johnson
Vice President, Sterling E-Marketing

Rich Merkouris is deeply passionate about making an impact for the Kingdom of God. He is a man of integrity who locks into a God-given vision and mobilizes people to make a difference for eternity. Rich's leadership is highly respected. He is a dynamic teacher with a message that is clear, practical and transformational.

Linda Outka
Coach, Speaker, Trainer, Author
Breakthrough Solutions

The passion Rich has for Christ is genuine, inspiring and contagious. His teachings have challenged me to be more intentional as I strive to live out God's word at home and at work. If you want a fluffy message of "I'm just fine and I can have God on my own terms," you need to go elsewhere. If you desire to really learn the Bible, purposefully grow in your faith and to stretch yourself to be a true disciple of Christ...you've found great place to start.

Darren Hefty
Co-Host of Ag PhD TV and Radio
Co-Owner of Hefty Seed Company

I've always appreciated Rich Merkouris' heart for the Kingdom of God. Rich is one who lives out what he preaches. He does what all good leaders should do: spends his days equipping others to do the work of the ministry.

Zach Bauer
Lead Pastor, Red Door Church

Over the last decade I have watched Rich launch several successful ministries. He has a rare ability to get a group of key leaders moving in the same direction. After participating in one of these groups, I understood what attracts so many people to serve beside him. It is the way Rich passionately follows Jesus, living every moment of life in service to others.

Nate Helling
Chief Financial Officer
Vice President of Operations
Sioux Falls Seminary

REAL LIFE

HOW TO LIVE WITH CONTENTMENT, CONFIDENCE, AND JOY

REAL LIFE

RICH MERKOURIS

THRONE
PUBLISHING GROUP

Cover Design: Caitlin Pisha
Lead Writer: Angela Tewalt
Editor: Cameron Brooks
Proofing Editor and Publishing Manager: Amy Rollinger

Throne Publishing Group
2329 N Career Ave #215
Sioux Falls, SD 57107
ThronePG.com

DEDICATION

I want to dedicate this book to my grandfather, Richard Peterson. He was a freight train of contentment, confidence, and joy, despite difficult circumstances of being in a wheelchair for twenty years. I'm forever grateful for his influence in my life and that I get the honor of carrying on his name.

TABLE OF CONTENTS

PART THREE:
The Path

INTRODUCTION

I've had the opportunity to spend years with Christians in my time as a pastor and ministry leader. As a law enforcement chaplain, I've also been in intimate relationship with people who are in the midst of hardship—some in the worst possible situations. And one thing I've noticed amid all those encounters is a familiar pattern: A lack of contentment, a lack of confidence, and a lack of joy.

Suddenly, I found myself wondering, how in the world is it that these people do not seem to be experiencing what the Bible teaches should be a lifetime of contentment, confidence, and joy? Where did we go wrong?

I believe there is another way. I believe God has a vision for us that lacks nothing and instead is full of His presence and promises; but this is not our reality. I am sensing that, for the majority of Christians—and even the majority of the world—this is not reality. And it can be. I pursue this vision because I believe we all desire contentment, confidence, and joy.

When you are in relationship with God, you experience a newfound freedom that no longer demands anything but instead exudes grace. This freedom gives you strength, resolve, and a willingness to live. You'll have a new appreciation and desire for community, prayer, and the Bible. You'll be disciplined but in need of nothing, and your spirituality will no longer be transactional but relational—intent on God's presence in your life. Let's explore this freedom by establishing a vision, dealing with reality, and then traveling a new path. And let's go together.

PART ONE

THE VISION

CHAPTER ONE

LIVING WITH POWER

I have a vision in my mind and on my heart. I think that when one has contentment, confidence, and joy, they are a freight train.

Indulge me for a moment with this picture in your mind, too.

A freight train is strong, heavy, and impactful. It is one speed, one direction, one way. And no matter what lies ahead, amid all the mountains and all the valleys, it moves forward mightily without hesitation and with great strength.

A freight train delivers. It delivers consistently, on time and every time. Nothing stops its delivery. It is reliable, steadfast, and powerful.

In this vision, *you are the freight train*. With contentment, confidence, and joy, you deliver the impact. You are strong, consistent, reliable, and mighty.

You can be the freight train.

This vision I have is counter-cultural, because we are not one-directional. We live life *this way* and *that way* and any which way on any given day. Consistency and reliability are not necessarily descriptors of us. I know this, but I also know that we are capable of being a freight train in the middle of this roller coaster of life.

Much like my vision of the train, I see our experiences in life as the roller coaster. There are extreme ups and downs and different speeds, and it's a very hectic ride, but we, as followers of Christ, can be the freight train in a world of roller coasters.

A roller coaster is not reliable, but your freight train will always deliver.

A freight train is also not easily derailed. If there is a fallen tree on the track, the train will charge forward anyway. It is not going to be stopped. However, if there is a fallen tree on a roller coaster's track, you have yourself a serious problem! Actually, the slightest obstruction can derail the roller coaster. Similarly in life, the slightest comment at the water cooler can offset our entire day.

But with contentment, confidence, and joy, you are not the roller coaster. You are the freight train and you will continue on your way.

When you are a freight train, your impact is generosity. You are giving of your time, your talents, and your words of encouragement, comfort, or correctness. You are a messenger, and you are constantly delivering action.

As a mighty force, you are also free from peer pressure or keeping up with the Joneses. You are free from discontentment and instead full of energy, peace, and delight.

You are fully present. You are present with family and yourself, but most of all, you are present around people who are different from you. Without a willingness to be around people unlike you, there is no opportunity for impact. But you are a freight train of impact and influence.

Because of your confidence, you can be present with people who are different than you. One of the biggest challenges in the Christian community today is that Christians feel the need to huddle up with like-minded others. But what if our God wanted us to be with people who were not like us?

That is where your biggest impact is going to happen.

Here is an example. Your neighbors do not believe in God. You have supper together every few weeks, and one night, a conversation about heaven and hell comes up. And the conversation doesn't go that great. But you know what? They are still going to get invited to the Super Bowl party. Because even though you don't agree with their beliefs, disagreement does not end your relationship with them. You are present with them anyway.

You are a freight train, and their beliefs cannot derail you. You are content and comfortable enough in your own skin to know that you can still be with people who are different from you and not be changed. With confidence, you can fully love a person who is unlike you without needing them to change for you.

In the roller coasters of life, we become so nervous around those who are different from us. Not only do we worry what other people will think if they see us with a different crowd, we also worry that we might start believing the wrong stuff. So we avoid them alto-gether. But if we are a freight train of contentment, confidence, and joy, we don't avoid different people, we invite them over for dinner and we intentionally spend time with them.

There is no pressure, just positive impact.

When you slow down the chaos of roller coasters in your life and settle into the powerful consistency of a freight train, you become a magnet to others. People are drawn to you and your impact. You are steady, strong, and even-keeled.

You become this freight train when you move from a saturation of rules and religion to a desire for the glory of God. You are no longer centered on self. You are no longer centered on others or things. You are centered solely on honoring God, magnifying God above all else, and shining God's magnificence through you.

Religion asks, "How close can I get to the line without crossing it?" We think, as long as I don't do X, Y, or Z, I'm safe. But the question is not, "What can't I do?" The question is, "What can I do for the glory of God?"

Pastor John Piper wrote in his book *Seeing and Savoring Jesus Christ*, "We are all starved for the glory of God, not self. No one goes to the Grand Canyon to increase self-esteem. Why do we go? Because there is greater healing for the soul in beholding splendor than there is in beholding self."

Having contentment, confidence, and joy means that we become so overwhelmed with the greatness and glory of God that we no longer focus on self because God is the new center of our life. We practice genuine selflessness. And as our new focus, we don't look down to God through a microscope. Instead, we gaze up through a telescope and gasp at God's splendor.

When we are in awe of our almighty God, we become a freight train in motion, and we deliver an impact like no other.

CHAPTER TWO

THE BIG THREE

Contentment, confidence, and joy are states of being. They are not reflective of one's self or even *about* one's self. Rather, they reflect our relationship with God and of God's presence in our lives.

Contentment is being in a state of, "The Lord is my shepherd, I shall not want" (Ps. 23). Confidence is my identity in Christ, and joy is being in a state of "rejoicing in the Lord" (Phil. 4:4).

These three are absolutely related and interdependent on one another, because they are all fruit, and they are all based upon the promises and the presence of God. Together there is a synergy, a teamwork among them that helps us reach the pinnacle vision for humanity, which is God's desire for us to have contentment, confidence, and joy.

What does contentment look like? How can we tell when someone has contentment?

It's important that you are able to not only identify these states of being within yourself, but that you see them in others, too, because we want to encourage each other. These states of being are evident in the way we act, talk, or think every day.

So, what does contentment look like? It's having peace, and it's a state of not wanting. Contentment is about more than just acknowledging what you have. It's about being grateful for what you have and then trusting that you are able to live and operate within those possessions.

Contentment is removing from your life the statement of, "I need *this* for *that*." If you say to yourself, "I need X to be happy," or, "I will not have peace until I have X," then you are not content. If something or someone or any circumstance is a necessity for your peace or your joy or your hope, then you are not in a place of contentment.

There is not a simple formula for contentment. It is indeed a process and a journey, and it is complex. Psalm 23 says, "The Lord is my shepherd; I shall not want"—one of the most recognized passages of scripture—but are we listening and abiding to that? How do we function within that? How are you going to move to a place where "the Lord is your shepherd and you shall not want?" The answer to that is your pathway toward contentment.

Someone who has contentment exudes a certain level of comfort—a real rest within them—and they are not running toward something. There is absolutely nothing of need.

Another practical sign of contentment is someone who is fully present in relationship. Those who are discontent have a hard time being fully present, either because the person they are with has something they desire and they feel less than them, or the person they are with is not giving them what they "want" at that time. So there might be a position of superiority or inferiority in place, and, therefore, it's impossible to be fully present.

In our culture, this is very obvious. Everyone is always on their phone while in conversation. They are having a conversation with someone and assuming they are being attentive, but they are simultaneously texting or taking calls or even on social media. This is a sure sign of discontentment because they are in a position of needing something even in the face of relationship with someone else.

But contentment is not found in something or someone or anything tangible. Contentment is found in the presence and promises of Christ.

What does confidence look like? How can we tell when someone has confidence?

Confidence is having the courage to act. It is a deep, quiet, inner strength that allows me to act in boldness.

I do not have confidence if I need X to approve of myself. I do not have confidence if I need X to feel good. I have confidence when I have a peace within myself of my own capabilities *as they are*. I am at peace with who I am because I have the presence of Christ in my heart.

The confidence I speak of here is not self-confidence. This is not about being boastful or arrogant or thinking highly of oneself. Rather, it is practicing humility. When people think too much about themselves, that is a lack of confidence. Narcissism and big egos are an extreme lack of confidence, because that means confidence is dependent upon what others say or think about you.

The guy who walks into a room needing to declare how tall he is is not confident in his height at all because he has to remind you—and himself!

When we start doubting ourselves or feeling a need to compensate for ourselves, we become self-centered instead of God-centered. But it is not about what "I can do for me." It's about what *Christ* can do *through* me.

Many people in the church lack confidence. Gifted, talented people will think they are incapable of the smallest things. "Ahh, I don't know if I can be a greeter," or, "Something needs to be said here, but I don't know how to say it or I might say it wrong, so I better not say anything at all." Many Christians are defensive and lack confidence, so they create false fronts to protect themselves instead of focusing on relationship with Christ.

But those who have confidence don't need a front. Instead, they have a bold willingness to act and are not dependent on the affirmation of whomever or whatever. Instead of being afraid to speak up, they are willing and ready to speak a word of encouragement, truth, or comfort.

Another sure sign someone has confidence is when they can be in the presence of greatness and not think less of themselves. If you are listening to a great singer, you can enjoy the song and not think, "Gees, I'm a terrible singer," or, "I wish I had that talent." You actually leave thinking, "Wow, I really appreciate their vocal ability and talent. What a beautiful singer."

What does joy look like? How can we tell when someone has joy?

Joy is a fountain of gladness within. It is a state of happiness not dependent upon circumstance.

It is important to note that there is a difference between happiness and joy. Happiness is momentary, and joy is enduring. Happiness is not deep, and joy has depth. Happiness is circumstance-driven, and joy is an ongoing presence, no matter what. Happiness is fleeting and may come and go throughout any given day, whereas joy is stronger and everlasting.

You can tell someone has joy in their ability to celebrate with others. Someone who has joy is completely present in someone else's joy, and the celebration of someone else is not an inferior or superior thing. Simply, they are truly glad for others.

You also can tell if someone has joy by the way they express themselves. If they speak negatively or project gloom, they do not have joy. Someone with a joyful demeanor projects hope and happy thoughts. Joy is rejoicing always in the Lord Almighty.

What happens when we lose contentment, confidence, and joy?

Contentment, confidence, and joy are all fruit of our relationship with God. Contentment is fruit of "The Lord is my shepherd" (Ps. 23). Confidence is fruit of Christ in me, hope of Glory. And joy is fruit of connectivity to Jesus. But we begin to lose our contentment, confidence, and joy when we disconnect with the source—the presence and promises of God.

Loss of contentment

When we begin to put our attention on others— when our relationships are horizontal and there is no vertical relationship with God—we begin to lose contentment.

In America, we have the unique opportunity to interact with people of different socio-economic statuses.

We get to meet and build relationship with people who are both above us and below us. But that can create a negative focus. If your friends start going out two nights a week for supper, it becomes engrained in you that you, too, should be going out two nights a week for supper. If your friend joins a gym, you want to join a gym, too. Your focus is less on God and more on what someone else has and what you may not.

This is a loss of contentment because you have taken your eyes off God. And in America, this is the No. 1 way to lose contentment, to lose the awareness and the presence of God. We have the promise of "Fear not, for I am with you" (Isa. 41:10), yet the moment this promise is no longer seared or burning within you, contentment begins to leak out. If the promises of Christ are only read once a year versus on a daily basis, contentment will leak out.

To avoid this, I call it "remember-izing" the Bible. I don't think we have to memorize every word of the Bible, but I do think we need to "remember-ize" God's promises. Think of God's promises as a cough drop, something you are slowly sucking on as the promises ooze out and into your body. And the result of these promises constantly oozing into us is contentment, confidence, and joy.

When I continue to "remember-ize" God's promises and understand that they are for me, for my well-being and my eternity, the need for anything else is taken away.

Another sign that one may be losing contentment is the need to buy things. A mid-life crisis is a good example. Someone may declare, "Let's get into camping!" So they buy a camper and all the necessary supplies. But then a few months later, that's not fun anymore, so they sell the camper and buy a motorcycle. On a smaller level, it's a need for instant gratification. I need to buy a coffee, I need dessert, or I am suddenly asking myself, "What if I had this? What if I bought that?"

Restlessness is a warning sign, too. Whether you having restlessness in your sleep or restlessness in your heart, you are lacking contentment. Restlessness flows from inner worry or inner desire. Inner worry is about something, and inner desire is for something, both of which are in opposition of being in the state that God desires us to be.

Loss of confidence

You know you are losing confidence if you have doubt. You are losing confidence if you are fishing for compliments or affirmation. You lose confidence if you are looking for something to satisfy you or satiate a need. This is a slow drain. No one loses confidence overnight, but the more a lie becomes truth, the more confidence leaks out.

Loss of joy

You lose joy when you remove the functionality of God in your life, because our source of joy is the presence of God.

Just like in contentment, a warning sign that you are losing joy is when you need quick hits of gratification. You need to watch just one more episode of your favorite TV show because it takes you out of the real world and gives you just a dose of laughter or time to zone out. You need to feel happy if just for a moment, but that need is a sure lack of overall joy.

Another warning sign is negative talk. When someone is always seeing the negative side of things, that is flowing from a lack of joy deep within.

And most importantly, I would contend that you know you have lost joy if someone you care about is going through something great, and you can't be happy for them. You can no longer celebrate for them.

Mindfulness

Even though there will be seasons of struggle—even though we will face real issues in life—these three states of being will continue to work together to create the ultimate vision for humanity. Be aware of God's presence and God's promises in your life, or lack thereof, for that will bring you contentment, confidence, and joy.

PART TWO

THE REALITY

CHAPTER THREE

REAL ISSUES

God wants us to be content

He desires for us a life of not wanting more or less, but a state of satisfaction that is not dependent upon circumstance.

We see commands such as, "You shall not covet anything that is your neighbor's" (Exod. 20:17). The base of that command is not, "Do not want from them," rather, it's about contentment with what you have and where you are in life. It's about wanting less for yourself.

God's vision for us is a heart that's in a state of rest, not in constant motion for something else. We've all had our stomach turn at different times in life, wanting or grasping for something more. Instead, God wants us to release that grip. He desires for us pure contentment.

God wants us to be confident

He desires for us a willingness to act that flows from genuine confidence. He wants for us to be people of action, and action flows from confidence. Unfortunately, Christianity is seen as a neutral activity. We think, as long as we're not doing something bad, we're good. But the reality is that not only should we avoid bad acts, we have been created to do something good. Good flows from confidence.

Ephesians 2:10 says, "For we are his workmanship, created in Christ Jesus for good works, which God prepared beforehand, that we should walk in them." To do something, to say something, or to be somewhere—that all flows out of confidence. People who lack confidence rarely get engaged in anything because they are concerned about what people think about them or if they even have enough capability. They might even hesitate to do something as simple as volunteer at a homeless shelter, because they believe they don't have enough ability to do so.

Confidence is at the root of convicted actions, like to be on offense. However, I would say the majority of Christians are *on defense* most of the time—always protective and focused on what they are against or what they will say "no" to—and Christian impact does not come from a defensive posture. Christians are meant to act with confidence and heart, to *want* to go for it! The best baker doesn't use a measuring cup, and the heart of that is confidence.

Christians have primarily become defensive due to cultural shifts that have minimized their influence. Our decreasing influence in culture and politics is causing us to question our impact; therefore, we are hesitant to act. But God desires for us to be on offense, to look up and live freely, but we cannot do so without confidence. Our confidence should not flow from cultural effectiveness or political influence, but rather our identity in Christ.

God wants us to be joyful

Philippians 4:4 says, "Rejoice in the Lord always, again I say rejoice!" God commands this of us because He desires us, and joy flows from Him. He wants us to be joyful.

The one desire within us that's never spoken against in scripture is joy. I would contend that when anyone wakes up in the morning, they wake up wanting joy. They might not actually say it or even think it, but nobody wakes up in the morning and says,

"I hope today is horrible. I hope I am horrible today." No, instead, whether subconsciously or intentionally, we hope for joy in our day, and that is the one desire that is not governed at all.

The Bible cautions against many of the desires we experience in life. But nowhere in the Bible does it speak against joy. Nowhere does it say, "Beware, be careful, do not let this get out of hand," or that you shouldn't want to be happy or joyful.

In the Bible, there is absolutely no prohibition of the desire for joy, because God wants us to be joyful in every way.

The question is not, "Should I want to be joyful?" The question is about which pathway to take today to be joyful, and that's where God speaks His Word. The desire for joy is a natural reflection of God, and even though the pathway toward joy can be broken, the actual desire for joy can never be broken by sin.

Today, most people are not content. Most are not people of action, and there is more anxiety in the Christian world than there is joy.

But you were created to live in contentment. You are meant to act in confidence. You are here to feel joy. I want you to experience all these things because you were created to be a person of impact. You were created to make a difference.

And you can.

Find me a difference maker who is discouraged, depressed, or doesn't have confidence. Find me a difference maker who is pure envy. This cannot exist! Doing good as we were created to do cannot exist without true contentment, confidence, and joy, and all encouragements and discouragements you will find in this book will lead to this simple yet mighty truth:

God desires for you to have contentment, confidence, and joy in your life. This is the vision for humanity.

What are real issues?

Even though this is the ultimate vision, we all experience real issues in life. A real issue is not an academic idea, but a mental, emotional, spiritual, or physical experience that every person has on a day-to-day basis. This can be loss, grief, guilt, mistakes, or a feeling of inadequacy. It's not about what's right and wrong. It's just reality. Real issues happen every day.

It's important to acknowledge these real issues, because ignoring them leads to apathy or a low drain of our spiritual fervor. If the Christian walk is meant to be something that exists *within* our day-to-day life, then surely that must include these experiences. Without an acknowledgement of the issues we naturally go through in life, our Christian walk would be something segmented or compartmentalized outside of everything else.

And it shouldn't be.

I would contend that real issues affect one's understanding of Christianity and perception of God more than their one-hour Bible study or one hour of worship each week. I think that's reality. Whatever I experience this week definitely affects my perception of God more than what I hear on Sunday morning. It's because real issues and how we feel about them are one of the biggest influences on our life. So we must talk about these things.

Real issues can refine and shape us so we cling tighter to that which is true, that which is our hope. These issues not only help us to relate well with others, but to have a positive impact in the world as well. They give us a level of understanding and allow us to be an instrument in someone else's life when they encounter a real issue of their own. Real issues can be seasons of preparation, as much of life is.

But real issues can derail us in a hurry because they can create a conflict between *what I believe* and *what I experience*. And unfortunately, what I experience is probably going to trump what I believe, thereby minimizing my belief, stealing my confidence and forcing me to look elsewhere for hope. Without confidence or contentment, there is no joy.

Here's an example. I believe that my God is a good, good Father. But I am going through this real issue of not having X. And if I don't have X, my God must not be a good, good Father because a good, good Father would provide this for me. I'm saying my God is good, but I'm secretly having a hard time believing it because I'm not getting what I want, need, or deserve, right? And once you get into this zone—where your belief and your experience conflict—you start to feel badly, yet you're having a hard time articulating that because you don't want to appear less religious to others, so you end up stuffing it a little bit. You hide from others what you are feeling. And while stuffing it away, you're lowering your belief almost secretly. You don't allow yourself an authentic community of friends to whom you can say, "You know what, it doesn't make sense to me why my God isn't providing X for me." You don't want to say that because you don't want people to perceive you as a less-than Christian. Suddenly, this endless cycle of not acknowledging how you feel becomes a slow rot of what you once believed.

I see this a lot in the chaplain world. When someone loses a family member, and I have to deliver the news of a death, it's not as if in that moment they immediately deny God exists. Instead, it's a slow rot of their faith that takes place over the next year. It begins with not wanting to go to church anymore because when they go to church, they are reminded of their late spouse because friends show up with their spouses. Then, the people at church don't see them at church for a while and they grapple with whether they should call. After a year of this, even though they've pulled back from community for what were legitimate reasons, they now don't have a place to express what is happening between their beliefs and their experiences. And over time, they are OK with it. They think, *I'm getting by going to church once a month*, and they don't even realize how much the experience—the real issue—has taken root, and belief has completely fallen away.

Another example is guilt. Say I make a mistake—I mistreat someone or I say something I shouldn't have said. Guilt sets in, but I never really deal with it or the individual I hurt, so that guilt just simmers. It creates a view of myself as less-than. And when I have a lot of guilt, I approach God less because I'm ashamed. After a while, guilt produces shame. So I'm embarrassed to face God and I'm not going to talk with Him as much.

This begins a slow rot. Over time, I'm doing my devotions only once a week as opposed to four days a week like I used to. I've lost my daily encounters, and I'm no longer building my confidence. The source of my contentment and joy is to "Rejoice in the Lord always" (Phil. 4:4) and find the Lord in the Bible, but guilt has washed that away. I've lost my connection.

It's a cycle that's barely visible; it creeps so slowly. But it can completely rob us of our belief if we are not aware.

As you seek contentment, confidence, and joy, you must confront the real issues in your life. Real issues do not make you less-than; real issues are simply a part of life for every single one of us. In the Christian world, we think we're not supposed to have real issues just because we have faith, but the reality is, Christ leaves us in a broken world and we are a broken people. As broken people in a broken world, we should not be surprised that real issues are still at play. Of course, there is an element of mystery here. Why doesn't God just fix it, then? The Bible reveals that God is working *through* His people, and it will all be fixed in one ultimate time that is simply not yet here in fullness. Until then, we must have an expectation that, with broken people in a broken world, there will continue to be challenges and difficulties.

But you can still rejoice. You can still do good.

CHAPTER FOUR

BAD ANSWERS

In the midst of real issues, we often encounter bad answers. A bad answer is a statement, an excuse to your problem, an "explanation" to what ails you. A bad answer is unhelpful. It is a declaration that is unfaithful to what God has made known about Himself and His purposes. A bad answer does not produce what God desires to produce. Rather, it produces action in the opposite direction or takes you along the wrong path.

A bad answer is one that contains a *kernel* of truth but doesn't give a helpful understanding and can create a harmful perspective as well. A bad answer doesn't need to give a full explanation, but it does create an avenue to a bad one.

Simply put, a bad answer could never be found clearly articulated in the Bible. It will be inconsistent with what God has made known to us in His Word. Sure, it may be connected to a *sentence* of the Bible, but it is not consistent with the *overall teaching* of the Bible. If the overarching goal is to bring God glory by reflecting the image of Jesus Christ to the world, then any answer that does not produce the image of God within us or among us is a warning sign.

Even though a bad answer may feel good to believe in—it may lift a burden for a moment—it does not reflect the character or the purposes of God, and it is unhelpful.

When we go through real issues, rarely do we find clean-cut and simple solutions, because real issues are messy! But bad answers are almost always short and simple, and that means you are not getting the best answer, and you surely aren't getting support from the person who gave you the bad answer. A bad answer is flippant and ignorant, and it is not supportive.

But bad answers exist anyway, because we live in a culture that wants a quick and easy way toward a God with whom they can agree with.

Bad answers also come from hurt people who have not dealt with their own hurt. If a person loses a loved one and doesn't deal with it, that transpires to the next person. If a person is emotionally or spiritually hurt by someone else and doesn't come to a place of reconciliation with them, that just gets passed down. If someone is hurt by wealth, they are going to perpetuate a notion that wealth in Christianity is bad. And we don't want to offend a hurt person, so we let them get away with their bad answers. Then, that bad answer takes root and keeps moving.

Let's unpack some bad answers:

"God needed another angel"

When people suffer a loss, they often hear, "God needed another angel." But this bad answer misunderstands the hope of the Christian. It dilutes the ultimate promise of Christianity: a resurrected body in an everlasting new Kingdom. The moment that this thinking of "God needing another angel" enters, it removes the necessity of the resurrection, thereby removing the necessity of Jesus. It also removes my hope.

A big issue in American Christianity is that we've removed the resurrection due to our misunderstanding of the afterlife. Our future is not an existence as a spirit, but rather a fully redeemed (resurrected!) creature. Our hope is a brand new body that is undefiled, not rusting, not fading. That all takes place when Jesus returns to establish the New Heaven and New Earth that exist for eternity. Any teaching that removes our focus on that as our hope is an unhelpful answer in that it does not give the fundamental teaching of the Bible.

Second, this bad answer lowers God, suggesting that He needs something from us. God doesn't need anything. Even though you are not saying that in the statement, when you sit with it for a while, you can't help but produce that type of thinking. It takes root and slowly begins to build this false perception of God.

"God needed another angel" also doesn't get to the hardship of death. Death is real and final. But on a biblical level, this statement completely misunderstands the angelic realm with the human realm. Human beings are different from angelic beings in that humans are actually above angels, and we bear the image of God. But this answer defies that.

We wonder why the Christian church doesn't have hope? It's because we've taken away the primary source of hope, which is the resurrection of Jesus.

"God needs your money"

This is a bad answer because it lowers God to a position of dependency, that God will only get X done if He has your money. And this is completely untrue. God's work can continue without your money.

Second, this bad answer elevates you, because the moment you give your money, you've supplied something that "God needed." It moves the giving from a place of joy to a place of pride. "God needs your money" can either create a sense of inferiority if I believe it and I'm not tithing, or a sense of superiority when I do tithe.

Most importantly, this answer frames money as "your money," which completely removes the fundamental understanding that Christian stewardship is about us managing *God's* money. We are not in a healthy place until money is money. Whenever money is something else besides that, we are in an unhealthy spot. A healthy spot is where money is simply money and I can release it freely. It is not controlling me, and I am managing it on behalf of God, flowing freely.

"Everyone makes mistakes"

I would contend that we give the answer, "Everyone makes mistakes," because we want to make God more approachable and loving. If someone does something wrong, we hear this all the time. "Hey, don't worry about it, everybody struggles with that. It's OK!"

Giving that answer allows you to avoid the biblical answer, which is, "That was a mistake, and that dishonored God." But saying flippantly, "It's OK, everyone makes mistakes," also removes the ultimate blessing of the Bible of God, which says, "I saw your mistake, but I'm not holding that mistake against you. *I forgive you.*"

To me, there is much greater joy that comes from a God who is aware of my mistake and doesn't hold it against me than a God who ignores my mistake or is unaware of it!

"Everyone makes mistakes" takes away the responsibility of forgiveness. We know that if we have to say, "I forgive you," we are also declaring to them, "I know you've done something wrong." And that can be offensive to the receiver! So, of course, to avoid making others feel worse about themselves, we use this bad answer to "fix it." But that does not deal with the root issue of the guilt that the mistake caused. The only thing that deals with the root of the mistake is to say, "I forgive you. I no longer hold that over you." And so often, we don't choose forgiveness. We choose neglect.

This bad answer is the most prevalent answer in the church and in the world right now, but it is completely offensive to the central message of Christianity, which is the forgiveness of sins. Whenever we say, "Everyone makes mistakes," as a follow-up to a wrongdoing, it takes away the necessity of Jesus and it removes the necessity of the cross. Second, it minimizes in a hurry the mistake and the standard. To say, "Everyone makes mistakes" is also saying, "It's no big deal." And if it's not a big deal, then why did Jesus die on the cross? It's a huge deal! And the fact that "everyone does it" doesn't make it right. We must acknowledge the mistake instead of lowering the standard or merely accepting, "It's happened before, and it will happen again. Oh, well."

"Everyone makes mistakes" implies that God doesn't see our faults. And if we believe that, we minimize God by assuming that He doesn't see our faults, and we minimize what is important in His heart. It is not good news to my ears to hear, "Don't worry about it. God doesn't see your faults." But it's really good news to my ears when I hear, "I see your mistake, and I forgive you."

If we say, "Everyone makes mistakes," God isn't praised in that. And if everything is done to the praise and glory of God, that statement does not lead the person who made the mistake to say, "Praise God, everybody is a sinner!" When I choose instead to say to someone, "In Christ, everyone is forgiven," the only response you could possibly muster is, "Thank you, God."

We must acknowledge our sins. We must not fall prey to bad answers. We should be disgruntled with our sin. Both Christians and non-Christians are in a state of sin. The difference between a Christian in sin and a non-Christian in sin is that the non-Christian is a reckless, flippant sinner. They might not even be aware of their wrongdoing, going along a path oblivious of sin. Whereas a Christian is not only aware of their sin, they are disgruntled and sorrowful in it, but eager to praise God for His forgiveness.

"God is in control"

This is the most difficult bad answer for me to discuss. I am even still wrestling with it, but I want to be honest with you in this book. I know some of you will disagree with me and even question my orthodoxy, which makes this all the more difficult, but I still find the topic important, and we need to go here. Together.

This answer is bad because it creates all sorts of assumptions and dangerous logical conclusions. On one hand, there is a kernel of truth in saying God is in control. But on the other hand, there is a kernel of something I would contend is *not* true—that God is controlling everything. But when one hears "God is in control" amid a difficult situation, they hear, "God is controlling everything." If your child is in a car accident and someone says, "God is in control," the receiving end of that is, "Well, God has an interesting way of controlling that driver who just hit my son." Yes, God does have the ability to step in anywhere and everywhere at any moment, but this statement creates a strong misperception of who God is.

My seminary professor illustrated it this way: "Having this mantra means that every time you slip on the ice, you get back up and think, 'Phew, glad I got that one out of the way!' It creates a mindset that God planned for you to slip on the ice—or that God planned for your child to get hit by a car—and that's not at all true."

A big negative effect of this statement is that it removes a sense of personal responsibility, which lowers our prayer life. What is the point of praying if everything is going to happen the way God wants it to happen anyhow? "God is in control" removes a level of intentionality.

For example, I have a ton of cavities. I drink a lot of Mountain Dew! But am I going to say, "Well, I was born with bad teeth, so I'm just not going to brush or floss that much because I know I'm going to have bad cavities anyhow!" The outworking is the same when we utter that God is in control.

The absolute beauty of God's creation begins to be lost when we flippantly declare that God is in control, because it creates a mindset of robotic engagement. There cannot be true love if it's only robotic engagement. Is it really praise or is it really love if it's all just manipulated activity? Additionally, it goes against what we see revealed in the Bible. Yes, there are moments in the Bible where God intervenes and acts and completely directs things down to the minute detail. But that does not mean that happens everywhere or every time. The narrative does not become the normative.

This is challenging to say because there is scripture that talks about how God knows the very number of hairs on your head (Luke 12:7), and not a sparrow falls without God knowing it (Matt. 10:29). We have to remember that we are finite beings trying to understand an infinite being. There is mystery. So, does God know I'm going to fall on the ice? Absolutely. But does God want me to fall on the ice? Of course not. It's revealed to us that God knows we are going to fall; but that should not logically mean He caused it. God knows all, but that does not mean God causes all. We must be confident in the mystery. Deuteronomy 29:29

says, "The secret things belong to the Lord our God, but the things revealed belong to us and to our children forever, that we may follow all the words of this law."

Moving forward

In the face of real issues, what is needed most is the real, ultimate hope of Christianity, which is the resurrection of Jesus, along with a persistent presence in people's lives. Outside of saying, "We are a broken people in a broken world," the best we can offer to others is our relationship. Just like a bad answer, no one wants to hear, "I'm here for you," during a difficult time, but in my chaplain experience, ninety percent of the battle is simply showing up. And families with whom I've worked will later come to me, not to say, "Thanks for saying what you said," but rather, "Thank you for being there."

I hate to mention Jesse Ventura in this book, but the former governor of Minnesota and famous wrestler once said something that has stuck with me. I'm paraphrasing, but he said, "Religious people use all this *stuff* as a crutch." And I think there is a kernel of truth in there of why we hang on to these "bad answers." We are just looking for a crutch to make it through. On one hand, the reason that "God needs an angel" sticks around is because it does provide a crutch for some people, in the sense that they can now think of their loved one as an angel. It's an easy excuse, but it doesn't allow us to live in the mystery of an omniscient God who's beyond us. Bad answers make God so relatable that we lose the magnificence of Christ.

Minimizing God eventually equals the loss of a magnificent God, without whom there is no contentment, confidence, and joy. Do not lose the magnificence of God.

PART THREE

THE PATH

CHAPTER FIVE

COMMUNITY

In scripture, we read that no one has ever seen God, yet God is made visible when we love one another (1 John 4:12). God has chosen to work *through* His people. We experience the presence of God when we are with the people of God.

And in order to be with the people of God, we need community.

If we say that contentment, confidence, and joy only come from the presence and promises of God, then the presence of God must be through the community of God.

It all starts with community.

True community is living in relationship with one another. It's encouraging one another, exhorting one another, caring for one another, forgiving one another, correcting one another, and loving one another at all times. In true community, when one part of the body hurts, the whole body is affected. When one part of the body celebrates, the whole body celebrates. It is the ability to share in one another's roller coasters and unite.

True community is authentic. Whatever is spoken is real—though authentic is not always good! I may be upset with you or hurt, but true community is expressing disagreement when there is disagreement, agreement when there is agreement, and all joys and all sorrows. In authentic community, the outward expression matches the inward thought.

True community is also equal amounts of giving and receiving. You cannot have community if you are always the giver and someone else is the receiver. It must be a two-way street! When we merely dispense, we create dependency. True community is both giving and receiving.

I will admit that true community is counter-cultural to our individualistic society, which is all about "me, myself, and I." We think spirituality is what "I" believe, when in reality, the Bible teaches us that spirituality is, by its very definition, relational, because *God is relationship.* God is Father, Son, and Holy Spirit, so "God" by its very term means relationship. We are created in the image of God; therefore, to reflect the image of God, we must be in relationship.

The overarching theme of the Old Testament is that God chose a *nation*, an entire group of people. In the New Testament, we see a greater emphasis on individuals coming to faith in Christ, but they, too, are grafted into a community called the church. Throughout the Bible is this sense of community and this conviction that *we are part of a people.* And community is not merely an opportunity; it is necessity. Not only is it commanded of us, but it's in the very nature and definition of God's desire for us.

Community is essential.

How does community create contentment?

In true community, you are no longer "keeping up with the Joneses." The Joneses are no longer people across the street or those revered from afar. Instead, the Joneses are now right there with you, next to you and a part of who you are. There is a strong sense of togetherness.

Contentment is not possible until you can be with others who have more than you and not be wanting. That takes time to achieve, but that is achieved in true community, and that type of community creates contentment.

How does community create confidence?

In an authentic, biblical community, you are going to be accepted for who you are, which allows you to get comfortable in your own skin. If you can't be yourself for fear of not being loved, you are not in true community. But when someone knows the worst about you and still loves you, it creates confidence within you, and that is true community.

How does community create joy?

Life is indeed a roller coaster. There will always be ups and downs, so you are going to need people who can go up and down with you—to empathize with you during your difficult times and to celebrate you during your happy times. This support is found in true community, and that kind of community creates joy.

How do you know if you are in true community?

You know you are in true community when you are spending time with people and you trust them. It is not always easy to ask for help, even in the small things. We've all been there, where we are afraid to admit we cannot do it alone. But this is part of life, and this is absolutely part of community. Asking for help is not a sign of weakness. It's a natural part of community that actually makes a group stronger. Yes, there is sometimes discomfort in honesty, but when you can depend on someone and, in return, let them know that they can equally depend on you, a new level of comfort is built, and a community becomes stronger.

Another sign you are in community is how willing people are to share. When you are amid a gathering of people, what is spoken about? If every prayer request is for someone else—"Please pray for my aunt," "Please pray for my friend going through X"—that shows a lack of comfort and a lack of trust. Whereas, if you can come into a gathering and say, "Please pray for my wife and me. We haven't had much alone time together and are having trouble communicating lately," or, "Please pray for my anxiety," that shows a huge amount of trust and commitment toward that community. But a lot of people in the Christian world haven't achieved this yet. Admittedly, it takes time to get there—to reach that depth of vulnerability—but it's amazing what happens when even one person initiates that step. Then the flood gates open and a true community really begins to grow.

Another sure sign of community is how often we are in one another's homes. For some reason, we have closed our houses to one another, which means we are closing our lives to one another. And how can you possibly be in pure relationship if you are never in someone's home, where they spend the majority of their life? We have professionalized hospitality. Can anyone even come to your house without two full days of prep anymore? When you get to that level of "professional hospitality," you begin to behave professionally with one another, too, and you lose that sense of authenticity.

Here's an example. We have a small group at our house who comes together often, and we eat supper together. We sit around our table, we eat, and then we move from supper into conversation, right there amid the dirty dishes. We don't finish our meal, disrupt the flow of conversation and say to one another, "OK, we are done with our meal, now let's get up and move into the study where we can talk about the Bible." That kind of behavior or expectation actually separates spirituality from real life. Instead, it all needs to flow together.

I thought a big celebration within our small group was when we were making shakes out of a blender after supper one night, and one of the guys just started drinking directly out of the blender. I remember thinking, *We have made it. He's at home. Now we've arrived.* That's a big deal, to feel that level of comfort within a community, but we've lost a ton of that! The pressure has become *so* high. How many people can just go play cards on Sundays anymore without needing to leave at a certain time, needing to be home at a certain time or needing to get the kids in bed at a certain time, right? There is a lot of false, fake pressure that has just invaded our relationships and, in turn, created nonauthentic community.

Loneliness is a major problem in our culture today, and I would contend a lot of that loneliness is a result of not opening our homes and our lives to one another as often as we should. A healthier culture begins with community, and how can we create an honest image of God if we are not in community with one another? If we are not in relationship, then we are not functioning according to our created being. True life is found in actually lifting someone else's burdens and realizing that we cannot bear our burdens on our own. To believe we could handle it all on our own is prideful, which is in opposition of God. But to share our burdens and vulnerabilities builds authentic community for which we were meant to live.

Forms of community

There are two forms of community: Formal and informal.

Formal community is an organized group of people that is structured. A process is in place, and you are prepared with what is going to happen there. It is familiar, consistent, and built into your lifestyle. A formal community also has authority that holds you accountable.

Sunday worship is formal community, as are Bible studies or weekly small groups. There is structure in place, an expectation and a consistent form of tradition that reinforces the value of the community. And this is what God designed for us. God designed for us to need one another in this form of community.

Informal community is non-structured, non-consistent, and without rules. Unlike formal community, this is a gathering of people that is more casual and intermittent, but still very important because it creates a new level of awareness of one another and therefore strengthens relationship, which strengthens formal community.

Informal community is having supper together, going on vacation together, watching football or going ice skating. These things may not be happening on a weekly basis, but they happen consistently enough that the relationship grows and flourishes.

In formal community, you can control yourself pretty well. You can come into formal community with a certain façade; your guards may be up. But informal community removes that. You can be more relaxed and open. And most importantly, you can understand the *whole you*. In formal community, the *whole you* can be protected very well, but in informal community, there is no pressure of performance or unspoken expectation, which, in turn, creates modified behavior. In informal community, you can take your guard down and relate with others.

Start with a formal community before you build an informal community. Each of us needs to be part of a church, but you can't *just* have formal either. If you only have formal, you won't have an opportunity to relate with others, and you will not have awareness of the "total you" with the total one another. Community is most rich when both are consistent and thriving. And when community is thriving, only then can you achieve contentment, confidence, and joy.

Action plan

How do you begin to achieve community? By finding groups that are one-on-one, midsize, and large.

1) One-on-one

Meet with somebody thirty to forty-five minutes a week just to read the Bible together, pray together, or talk about life. This is not a mentor—this is peer-to-peer, with no hierarchy, only equal ground. You need this because you need an outside voice looking *into* your life. The easiest person to lie to is yourself, so you need a consistent outside voice speaking honestly into your life.

2) Midsize

A midsize community provides those casual, realistic, relatable relationships. You can't have in-depth relationships in large community with 200 people, but you can have deep, meaningful relationships with twelve to fifteen people, and that is found in midsize communities. Midsize communities provide you an opportunity to connect with different people in different ways.

3) Large

Large communities are your consistent Sunday church services that provide a needed level of strength and structure.

In the healthiest of senses, these are all weekly engagements. I encourage a weekly worship experience, where you can engage, make yourself known, and become part of a larger body. And I would also encourage a weekly one-on-one experience because everybody needs the consistency of another's support and voice in their life. As for midsize, I would encourage a minimum of every other week—if you wait four to six weeks, that's too long of a gap in time to feel comfortable and be real with someone.

Please know, this is not a thirty-day diet plan. This is not a means to an end. *This is a way of life.* To have community is *part of the vision.* If you want to be the freight train of contentment, confidence, and joy, you begin with community.

It all starts here.

CHAPTER SIX

GOD'S WORD

Your next step in the pathway toward contentment, confidence, and joy is being in God's Word. I believe the Bible is God's Word, which is written revelation of God's character and purposes.

To me, the Bible is a mirror reflecting God's image. When I read the Bible, it is reflecting to me the heart and character of God and the purposes of God, and He has chosen this written Word as His way to communicate with us.

Sixteenth-century theologian Martin Luther once said, "The Bible is the cradle wherein Christ is laid." The Bible is our modern-day manger, where we meet Jesus. We didn't get to meet Jesus in Jerusalem in a literal manger, so for us, we meet Him in the Bible. The Bible is what makes Jesus known to us.

I revere the Bible above all others books because of its author. In any other case, I determine the value and worth of a book based on its content. But the Bible is different than any other book because the value is not determined by its content, but by its author. It is valuable and prized literacy because of who wrote it.

The Bible is also unique because it contains a variety of literary styles. It is vastly different than reading any other book because instead of one, consistent literary tone, it contains a variety of different voices in which God communicates to us. God communicates to us through poetry, historical writings, or letters. But this also means that Christians can get themselves into trouble by reading the Bible literally. And even though we should read the Bible literally, *we should listen to what the Bible literally teaches, not what the Bible literally says.*

For example, the Bible literally says the earth is flat. It says there are four corners, but that is not what the Bible is teaching. This is why it is important to understand that the Bible contains a variety of different human ways of writing, all within one book. It is a far deeper, more meaningful and authoritative book than we treat it. This is why I encourage Bible reading as intensely as I do, because it is so unique, and we have so much to gain from it.

God's Word doesn't just inform us. The goal of the Bible is not primarily information. Rather, the goal of the Bible is first, revelation—to make salvation known to us—and second, to do something to us, to shape us and form us. The true effect of God's Word is to equip me, train me, and comfort me. *The goal of the Bible is transformation.*

A key Bible passage says, "All scripture first made us wise for salvation, for teaching, for correction and for training in righteousness, that the man of God may be complete, equipped for every good work" (2 Tim. 3:16-17). The ultimate effect of God's Word is that it is going to shape me into the image of Christ. It is going to make God known to me and reveal God's promises. And to have joy and contentment, as we are seeking here, I need God's promises in my life. Those are all contained in God's Word.

This is not a magic eight ball

Most people do not treat the Bible correctly; they treat it as a magic eight ball or a map, wanting answers for their specific questions. But what you are doing in that scenario is putting yourself *over* God's Word. For example, you may open the Bible looking to read something about friends, so you go to the concordance to find where it talks about friends, then you put yourself *over* the Word and apply it to your life in whichever way pleases you. But there is danger in this, because if you treat the Bible like an encyclopedia, you will get bad answers like we talked about earlier in the book. Whereas, if you have the discipline of just being *in* the Word and methodically working your way through it, you place yourself underneath it and you cannot control what will come next. You allow the Word to speak to you.

God's Word is not a magic eight ball because we cannot ask it questions or speak to it to get what we want. It is far more general than that! The Bible *is* recordings of what God has done, will do or is doing, but it is *not* revelation of answers to every single question we have about life. The Bible may not give me what I want, but it will give me what I need.

The Bible makes known everything that is needed for a life of contentment, confidence, and joy. But that does not mean the Bible answers every question in life. Rather, the Bible equips us to answer our questions.

What process will you choose to live with the Bible? Most of us choose a process that is unfaithful to the

Bible simply by the way we mistreat it. But it is much more faithful to say, "I want to live *under* the Bible. I do not want to control it."

To me, if God's Word is written revelation of Himself and of His purposes, there is no other way to know Jesus Christ outside of the Bible. We encounter God through His Word. And if I want to have a daily encounter with God, it is only possible through the Word of God, because that is how God has chosen to reveal Himself to us. The creation tells us that there is a God. *But the Bible tells us who this God is and what this God desires.* This is why the Bible is the only way to know Christ.

Read, reflect, act

So often, we make the Bible about ourselves. We project its narrative onto our lives. But the Bible isn't about us. It is about the greatness of Jesus! Even still, people expect the Bible to lay out what they should do with their life and how they should do it. They expect God to make much of their life, when they should be asking, "What does this reveal about *God's* life?"

Try reading the Bible like this. After you read a passage, ask yourself these two questions before moving forward:

1. What is God making known about Himself?
2. What is God making known about His purposes?

Only after you ask and answer these two questions in regard to the passage can you ask, "How does this apply to my life?"

This will make such a tremendous difference. So often, people read a passage in the Bible and think, "Eh. That didn't have much to do with me today or what I am going through right now." And they close the book. But you miss a ton when you treat the Bible so selfishly! The biggest problem of all is that if you really think the Bible "didn't apply to your life today," then chances are you aren't going to pick the Bible up again, because it did not provide what you wanted.

Approaching the Bible with these two questions will change your expectation of what you are going to get. It removes any disappointment or unrest you once felt because you aren't expecting the Bible to be about you anyway.

However, the answers to these questions will reveal to you that *every passage* can apply to your life. For example, say you are reading a passage and it's obvious that God's purpose there is to build people up with our language. Then, if you took that purpose and implemented it into your everyday life, you would realize that God loves the unlovable, and that can be applied to your character. You may not have begun your time with the Bible thinking you needed to change your character or the way you treat people, but you leave your time with the Bible that day with the inspiration, revelation, and reminder to love all people.

It is overwhelming how much these two questions can change your time with the Bible.

The way I make the most of God's Word is to put the necessary work into it, and the necessary work is not looking for the quick and easy answer but *taking time to read, reflect, and act.* Most of the time, we go from read to act when a passage seems clear to us, but we don't reflect. However, asking the two questions forces you to reflect. If you want to get the most out of God's Word, then you must include time to reflect. You cannot just read and walk away because it is reflection that will lead to action. Reflection is where we discover, *How does my life align with the purposes of God?*

How will I know if my reflections are working?

When you begin the practice of reading *and* reflecting with the Bible, you will see change. Of course, you will have contentment, confidence, and joy, but moreover, you will gain a different perspective that is critical to having the promises of God—which brings you contentment, confidence, and joy. Most of us unfortunately live with a here-and-now perspective—what is right in front of me—but having a relationship with the Bible elevates our perspective beyond the here-and-now and to the eternal.

If I'm being honest, there is also going to be wrestling within you on different things. Even when you begin to submit yourself to the Bible as an authority, you will not always agree with what the Bible is teaching. But with that comes change. And if you have no change of mind whatsoever, then you have not been in the Bible as you should be. What are the chances that you completely align with everything God desires for us? Surely, there will be change in your opinions.

You also have to trust and allow that your culture will influence the way in which you read the Bible. Naturally, we come to the Bible with some sort of prejudice, but it is still possible to get to a point of maturity where you can ask, "Is my cultural understanding appropriate and faithful to the heart of God?" In America, this is admittedly difficult because we have bigger pride issues than almost any other country, but your cultural mindset can be changed.

For now, it's most important to understand that regardless of culture, *there is truth in the Bible that transcends every culture and every generation.* So when you ask what the Bible reveals about God and God's purposes, you are looking for an answer that would be the same in every culture, in every time, and in every place. And if what you've reflected upon is *not true* in every culture, in every time, and in every place, then you have not gotten to the heart of what God is trying to reveal in that passage.

It is a mighty destination to reach, but it is possible. Another way you know you've arrived to a healthy position with the Bible is when you can identify a tradition, a way of thinking, or a political position you once held that you changed. Moreover, if you can ask those two questions and then ask, "How does my worldview change as a result of this?" then you have grown. It takes a lot of maturity to get to a point where you can admit that the way you look at the world is wrong and then change it, but it is possible, and it is a true sign that you have been submitting to God.

All of this work takes time. An old man I used to have Bible study with once said, "The Bible has a shelf life of one day." We cannot live on yesterday's encounter or promises. We need fresh encounters and fresh promises every single day. Physically, we could not live on yesterday's meal. We'd be dragging all afternoon! We need a renewal of God's promises and a renewed encounter with our Creator every day. It is a relationship that deserves our consistent attention. The only way to walk with God in relationship is to be with God, and the only way to be with God is through His Word, so tend to that daily. This is the necessity.

Also, you need community as you work through God's Word. We all have cultural blind spots, so to make the most of your Bible reading time, it is best to have another person to see things you may not see or hear things you may not hear. We all come to the Bible from a very specific slant, and it's always good to have another slant to encourage or affirm or challenge our own way of thinking. Community is critical to Bible reading because it brings a level of protection to our interpretation.

With community and God's Word working together, we begin to succeed on the pathway toward contentment, confidence, and joy.

Action plan
1) Daily interaction
Every day, for seven minutes a day, intentionally work through the books of the Bible in a new mindset. If you miss a day, no one cares. Know that. There is no quiz at the end of the day. God does not take attendance, and if your relationship with God is dependent on that, you need to start over from the beginning of what it means to be a Christian. We are really good at talking about grace, but we are horrible at applying it. Give yourself grace.

2) Reflection
To break down your daily interaction, read the Bible for five minutes a day, and spend two minutes of reflection with these questions:

1. What is God making known about Himself?
2. What is God making known about His purposes?

Only after you ask and answer these two questions in regard to the passage can you ask, "How does this apply to my life?"

There is nothing special about seven minutes. It's simply realistic in our culture. Seven minutes a day can dramatically alter your relationship with the Bible, and you can work your way through a ton of the Bible in that short time.

3) *Where to start*

Do not read the Bible from Genesis to Revelation—from the front to the back—because that means you won't get to Jesus until September of every year! Rather, start in the New Testament in this order:

1. Luke
2. Acts
3. 1 Peter
4. Ephesians
5. 1 John

Once you've worked through these five, you will have built up a discipline, and then you will be ready to work through the rest of the Bible. From there, start in Genesis. Work your way through the Old Testament and then back into the New Testament until completion.

When you start with Luke, you start with the life of Jesus, who is the climax and the whole point of the Bible. The life of Jesus is the pinnacle of God revealing Himself to us. And those first five books give us a foundational understanding of the Christian life and the message of Christianity as a whole.

As you begin this journey, remember that the Bible will make known to you everything that is needed for a life of contentment, confidence, and joy. This is not done by answering all your questions or needs. Rather, the Bible *equips you* to answer your own questions. Treat the Word respectfully, and give yourself grace.

CHAPTER SEVEN

PRAYER

The final step in the pathway toward contentment, confidence, and joy is prayer. Prayer is conversation with God, us as humans talking directly to our Creator.

I want to be very honest and transparent with you here. I believe God speaks to us through the Word and that God's Spirit is given to us through the Word, but I personally have never had an experience where God has spoken to me. I have had experiences where people are speaking to me, and I know God is speaking *through* them to me, and I have also sensed at times that the Spirit is leading me to do X, but I have never had a two-way conversation with God. In prayer, I am making known to God my thanks, my praises, and my requests, but I have not heard from God in prayer. That has been my experience thus far.

Sometimes, I fear that people are driven away from prayer because of the guilt of not hearing from God. But I think we need to remember that prayer is God's gift to us! God has already spoken and is speaking and will speak through His Spirit with us. If your vision of prayer is two people at a coffee shop having a conversation together, then you may be greatly disappointed with your prayer life. It is much more one-way than that, as it is us *entering the presence of God*, making our praises, requests, and thanks known.

God's desire is for prayer to be a consistent presence in our life, not a dutiful religious expression once or twice a day. Even as a pastor and ministry leader, I do not spend three hours a day on my knees or in a chair praying. I never have. But I do believe that prayer is an ongoing communication with God *throughout* the day.

Let me put it this way: I am in a *spirit of prayer* twenty-four hours a day and in an *activity of prayer* numerous times throughout that twenty-four hour period. I am in a mindset and with the overall awareness that I can talk to God at any moment. And I think all of our prayer lives would change dramatically if we got more into the mindset that God is available to us at all times.

In Jesus' name

Here is how my day begins. Every morning, I intentionally put myself in a spirit of prayer by literally speaking, "in Jesus' name, we begin." I literally start the day in Jesus' name. Now, I might not finish every prayer throughout the day "in Jesus' name," but I have begun my day in that spirit. "God, good morning, thank you for this day. Today, I begin in Jesus' name, and I declare that access at any moment I need it. Thank you." I don't see the words "in Jesus' name" as a vital tagline that I must put on the end of every prayer. Rather, I see it as a spirit of access.

To say "in Jesus' name" means that Jesus is our High Priest, the One who gives us access into the temple. In the Old Testament, there were only a few people who were allowed into the temple and into the presence of God. Those were high priests, and the high priests went into the temple on our behalf. Then, in the book of Hebrews, it talks about Jesus now being our High Priest. Now Jesus goes on our behalf and provides continual access for us (Heb. 4), and any high priests before Him were foreshadows of Jesus to come. Once Jesus became the High Priest, there was no need for any others. This means that Jesus has provided for us the *ultimate and eternal access* through Himself. When I pray "in Jesus' name," I am saying, "I am coming to you, God, and all my requests to you, God, are based upon Jesus as my High Priest."

Think of it as name dropping. We do this all the time. We call a stranger and say, "Hey, I got your name from X," or we apply for a job and say, "X sent me." We are implying, "I know this person, so I'm in, right?" To declare, "in Jesus' name" is the exact same thing. We are saying, "God, I am coming to talk to you right now, and I am not asking that you listen to me or grant my requests *because of who I am*, I am asking and coming to you *because I know Jesus*. He is my High Priest, and I would not be bold enough to come to you without Him because I know I wouldn't even be allowed here."

To be clear, declaring Jesus does not mean that your requests will automatically be granted; it just grants you access to God and God's ear. Declaring Jesus gives you the *opportunity* for conversation.

The whole point of praying "in Jesus' name" is that it gives you access to God the Father. There is no access to God the Father without Jesus. When Jesus taught us to pray in His name (John 14, 15), He wasn't flippantly giving us a tagline to turn all our requests into a Christian prayer. *He was teaching us the way of prayer.* He was telling us that we now can approach God *because* of Him. We have access to God the Father *through* Jesus, so when I say every morning, "I begin this day in Jesus' name," it creates in my mind what I call VIP access to God.

VIP status is based off something, right? Maybe you donated a lot of money or you know someone or you are in a position of authority. And in this case, the basis of our VIP is Jesus. Only those who are connected to Jesus are given the VIP access to God.

The dilemma

I want to acknowledge something we rarely talk about openly in the church: the issue of unanswered prayer. The very fact that I bring up the *possibility* of unanswered prayer I know will bother some of you, because you think I'm being unfaithful in even suggesting it. But in prayer, we must also accept and speak to the mystery that is taking place here.

In the Bible, we read, "Ask, and you shall receive" (Matt. 7:7). Yet we all know that we do not receive everything we request. We know God hears us and wants us to speak to Him, yet we must acknowledge that there is mystery in God's response. When we are in the Bible, we are not asked to work our way down the logical ladder. We are asked to work our way down what has been revealed or made known by God. And what is made known is that God hears us and God desires to hear us. What has *not yet been made known* is why some requests are granted and why some are not, but granting does *not* mean that what did not happen was God's will.

This is a slippery slope because with unanswered prayers can come a bit of shame, guilt, and a slowing of prayer life. For example, if you pray, "God, heal X," and it doesn't happen, then you are less inclined to pray for Y or Z. You think to yourself, "If God cannot grant something as big as healing, then why would I pray for something less-than and expect it to be granted?" Unanswered prayers can create doubt, and doubt leads to inactivity and less prayer. But this all goes back to the overarching purposes of God. If I understand and believe the overarching purpose of eternity, and I'm saturated with conviction of the resurrection and a new kingdom forever, it can really change the effect of any circumstance here and now in my life.

Here is an example. Someone calls me up and tells me that I just won $1 million, but I have to pick it up in fifteen minutes or it's gone. Wow! OK, I will definitely be there in fifteen minutes! But, as I get up to drive there, I realize my wallet is missing. Am I going to spend fifteen minutes searching for my missing wallet? Of course not. I'm going to get in my car and pick up the money! Because, all of the sudden, even though a missing wallet can be a big problem, the promise of $1 million makes the missing wallet seem pretty minimal!

If I am so saturated with the promise of God, the resurrection and *life eternal*, any circumstance I face does not seem as monumental. Or, if a circumstance I want to improve does not improve, I am still at peace because at least God's overarching purpose has not been thwarted. Despite my unanswered prayer—despite any circumstance that may hurt—at least God's overarching purpose of *life eternal* remains. Yes, that is very hard to hear in the moment, but this is how we come to understand the presence and promises of Christ.

How will I know that God hears my prayers?

In the Word, God promises that He hears our prayers. The rest of it comes back to Jesus' name. You can have confidence in the power of your prayers because you are not asking on your own goodness. You are asking in Jesus' name, and there is no higher name than the name of Jesus. God the Father has given Jesus full authority over everything, and if we come to the Father through the One who has full authority, then we can have confidence that we have access and that we are being heard.

Just like the guilt I mentioned earlier that some people may feel if they don't hear God, others may feel guilt and shame because of personal failure. If I know I did something wrong and I know God is aware of what I did, I may be reluctant to come to God in prayer because I am ashamed. But Jesus' name changes all of that. Coming to prayer is no longer dependent on how good or bad I have been. We should not come to God saying, "Well, it's been a good day, so I can talk to you now." Or, on the contrary, "God, it's been a bad day, or I am going through something difficult, so I need to talk to you now." Our access should not be dependent on that. Rather, we come to God because of Jesus.

We base our prayer with God off of Jesus. And that needs to become *engrained* within us. It needs to be *branded* in our prayer life that *conversation with God is not based off ourselves or our performance in life*. It is based off Jesus and Jesus only. If my prayer life is based off my performance, my conversation with God will be highly limited and, frankly, volatile. But when it is branded in me that my conversation with God is based off the authority of Jesus, everything will dramatically change and my prayer life will feel free.

Your prayer life—and this entire journey—should feel liberated and free.

The model of prayer

In Luke 11, Jesus was asked, "Can you teach us how to pray?" Scripture says, "Now, Jesus was praying in a certain place, and when he finished, one of the disciples said to him, 'Lord, teach us to pray, just as John taught his disciples'" (v. 1).

What was Jesus' response? He recited to them what has become known as the Lord's Prayer.

In this answer, Jesus was not saying that whenever they prayed, they had to recite the Lord's Prayer. Unfortunately, some groups today take that answer as such. They feel they have to recite the Lord's Prayer, word for word, every single day. Even though there is nothing wrong with that—you can surely say the Lord's Prayer anytime you want!—there is nothing right with that either. What Jesus was teaching—what the Bible was teaching, not saying—is that the Lord's Prayer is a guide *to what we should be praying about.* This prayer is a model of themes we should focus on when we pray to God. If you feel guilty about wanting to talk to God but not knowing what to say, Jesus guides you by saying, "Here, look to this prayer, and then you will know what to pray about."

Let's break it down:

"Our Father, who art in Heaven, hallowed be thy Name"

This line is saying, "God, you are awesome!" We start our prayer by declaring that God is holy and perfect. Let us start all our prayers with a focus on God's greatness.

"Thy Kingdom come, thy will be done, on earth as it is in heaven"

Always acknowledge the plans and purposes of God's ways. This is encouraging us to pray big! We are asking for God's purposes to be accomplished in us and through us.

"Give us this day our daily bread"

Jesus is reminding us that it's OK to ask that our daily needs be met. This is such a practical thing but it is vital to a continued relationship with God. It's OK to tend to our needs!

"And forgive us our trespasses, as we forgive those who trespass against us"

In prayer, we must always ask for forgiveness of our sins. Freely ask God to restore and renew your relationship with Him. In this portion of the prayer, we are also asking for the ability to extend to others what God has extended to us, which is forgiveness.

"And lead us not into temptation, but deliver us from evil"

We should always be asking God to protect us from evil, but also make us aware of evil in this spiritual battle we are in every day. Grant me awareness as I live my life.

The Lord's Prayer addresses everything we need to build a healthy relationship with God. To look within its words is to receive freedom to talk honestly with God, to be God's friend! Do not be afraid to have real conversation with your Almighty Creator.

Religious activity can give us a false sense of security. We can recite the Lord's Prayer daily, over and over, but that rote can give us a false sense of security about our true, spiritual well-being. When, in reality, if we only recite the same prayer over and over, we rely on those words and think we are good to go. But are you able to express to God? If you cannot express anything and everything honestly to God, to speak spontaneously and unscripted to God, then you do not yet understand the nature of the relationship that God desires to have with you. Find me a healthy relationship in life based on routine and memorized words. It is not possible, because you need informal, real, honest conversation to create meaning and true love.

Action plan

1) In Jesus' Name

I encourage you to use the declaration of "in Jesus' name" throughout the day in your prayer life. Build those words to become a habit, to become so engrained in you that you do not even consider coming to God with your own good or bad, but with Jesus.

2) The Lord's Prayer

Use it as a guide to your conversation with God. Then, find your own words that you want to say to God. Speak to your own necessities and to your own sins and to your own fears of evil, and begin to build the relationship God desires to have with you. The Lord's Prayer is a guide for you, but your relationship with God is not governed by rules or expectations or how often or when or where you pray. Free yourself from any assumption and express yourself to God.

CONCLUSION

Most of us do not experience the fullness of a Christian life because we seek to be in control rather than submit our lives to Jesus. We assume that having control of our life is what gives us freedom, but the truth is the opposite. *Freedom is found in relationship with God.* Freedom is in relinquishing control and giving our lives to God. Freedom is in the pursuit of a vibrant, beautiful, and intentional spiritual life with Christ.

My hope is that you have accepted my challenge and that you have pursued this new path with God. My hope, too, is that these chapters have provided for you a greater sense of freedom and a renewed desire to greatly pursue a life with God. I hope I have not only given you a vision of what God desires for His Kingdom, but that you also feel empowered to begin your own path toward contentment, confidence, and joy.

I hope you have realized by now, *Why wouldn't I want this for my life?* Why wouldn't you want this for your life?

This journey takes time. Your freight train is on a long trip, but it is worth every mile because the promise of life eternal awaits you. What we have talked about in community, Word, and prayer is not a formula. It is a disciplined pathway guided by intention, patience, honesty, and consistency, but in all of that, there is freedom.

When you seek contentment, confidence, and joy— when you seek the presence and promises of God in your life—you are free.

May you be free.

ABOUT THE AUTHOR

Rich Merkouris is the Pastor of King of Glory Church in Sioux Falls, South Dakota. Rich helped start King of Glory in 2010 with the goal of mobilizing a group of people to journey together for the glory of God.

Alongside his duties as Pastor, Rich serves as the Chairperson for the Board of Directors of the Sioux Falls Ministry Center and Compassion Child Care. Rich also serves as the Director of Operations for the Kingdom Capital Fund in Sioux Falls.

He is passionate for seeing people become generous stewards of God's resources and giving fervently toward evangelism and mercy ministries.

Most importantly, Rich is the husband of Shannon and father of Hannah, Henry, and Hazel. His family enjoys opening their home to guests from church or the community. Rich's passion is to see people experience true community by opening their lives to one another, which requires being in one another's homes.

ABOUT THE COMPANY

King of Glory Church is a non-denominational church that exists to glorify God. The focus of the church is to build relationships, learn God's Word, serve the world and share the good news of Jesus Christ. These focuses are accomplished through intentional teaching during worship on Sunday morning, community groups for people to belong and city love teams where people are engaged in serving.

King of Glory met in a variety of locations before moving into their current location, an old lumber yard. The simple facility is a reflection of their desire to keep the focus on mission and ministry rather than facilities. There is a large focus on partnering and supporting ministries that are doing God's work locally and globally. Partnerships exist with mission groups in Mongolia, Liberia, Jamaica and Sioux Falls.

All ages participate in the life of the church with specific programming available for children and students on Wednesday nights. The overarching desire of the congregation is to see God glorified as people come together to learn, serve and share.

Website: kingofglorysf.org
Office: 605-271-3456
Email: info@kingofglorysf.org
Facebook: facebook.com/kingofglorysiouxfalls
Address: 1001 E. 17th St.
Sioux Falls, SD 57104